The Amazing Incredible Shrinking Violin

Story by Thornton Cline
Illustrations by Susan Oliver

ISBN: 978-1-57424-313-0
SAN 683-8022

Cover by James Creative Group

Copyright © 2015 CENTERSTREAM Publishing, LLC
P.O. Box 17878 - Anaheim Hills, CA 92817

www.centerstream-usa.com

"Such a beautiful story. It brought back a flood of wonderful memories when you taught my son."

– *William Lee Golden of the Oak Ridge Boys*

"Entertaining, empowering, and sure to make you smile! *The Amazing Incredible Shrinking Violin* will motivate even the most stubborn amateur. Cline's book makes practice fun; combining practical etudes, prose, and poetry in this musical fairy tale of *use or lose.*"

– *Jennifer Stirling, Lindsey Stirling Executive Assistant*

"This story is fun, creative, and clever with a strong and positive message for today's young children."

– *Crystal Bowman, best selling children's author.*

"Though I've never been too musically inclined, Thornton Cline's delightful book makes me wish that I'd practiced my clarinet more when I was a young girl. I believe children will relate to this story and benefit from the lesson woven into the text–practice truly does make perfect."

– *Michelle Medlock Adams, Award-winning children's author of more than 70 books.*

The Amazing Incredible Shrinking Violin

Ever since Austin was two years old, he had dreamed of playing the violin. He imagined himself on stage in the spotlight with a large crowd wildly cheering him. Austin begged his parents for a violin. Some of his friends played fun songs in a violin class at school. Austin wished to join them. Finally, his parents got Austin a red shiny violin.

Austin was so happy his parents signed him up for violin class.

"Austin you need to remember to practice every day," his parents said. Austin was so excited that he couldn't wait to show everyone his new violin.

He told everyone, "One day I'm going to be a big star on the violin!"

His teacher, Ms. Jackson welcomed Austin to class.

"This is how you hold your violin and bow," she said. His first song was "Twinkle, Twinkle Little Star". Ms. Jackson told the class to go home and practice.

When Austin got home from school his parents reminded him, "Austin, don't forget to practice."

Instead, he played with his baby sister, played video games, watched television and did his homework.

He did everything but practice.

At each violin class, Ms. Jackson would ask him if he had practiced. Austin shrugged his shoulders and said, "I don't have time to—I'm too busy."

Ms. Jackson replied, "now Austin you must find the time to practice if you want to sound good."

Austin didn't listen to his violin teacher. Weeks passed and he never practiced.

One night after his parents had tucked him into bed, Austin couldn't sleep. Suddenly, a bright light startled him. A tiny woman with wings and a wand appeared. She wore a dress all covered with golden violins. Austin thought he was dreaming.

The woman said, "Don't be afraid. I am the violin fairy. You have been given a special gift. You have a beautiful violin and talent. But you do not practice as you should."

Next she waved her wand over Austin's violin and  case which was sitting in the corner of his room. Austin stared at her with his mouth wide open.

The violin fairy said, "I have sprinkled fairy dust on your violin. Every day you do not practice, your violin will shrink. And one day, it will vanish."

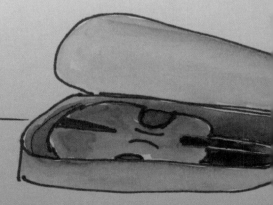

The tiny fairy disappeared. Austin lay in bed staring at the ceiling for a long time until he fell asleep.

The next day in violin class Austin thought about what the violin fairy had said. He laughed for he thought it was a dream. It was the end of class and his violin hadn't changed sizes.

All that week Austin didn't listen to anyone. At home, he did everything, except practice. When Austin returned to Ms. Jackson's class to play, some of his classmates couldn't stop laughing.

"Look at Austin's violin!" said a student. "It shrank!"

Austin showed his violin to his classmates. They called Austin's violin the "amazing incredible shrinking violin." All of the students wanted to see it. They said that it should be in the Book of World Records as "the amazing incredible shrinking violin."

Weeks passed, Austin still hadn't practiced. Every time Austin would play his violin in Ms. Jackson's class he would squeak, scratch and sound really bad. All of the other violin students were getting so much better than he was. His violin had shrunk so much that it was almost impossible to play. Austin felt like quitting and never coming back to Ms. Jackson's class. His classmates were making fun of him and Ms. Jackson wasn't happy that Austin wasn't improving.

Austin started wishing he had practiced. He wished he had listened to his parents, Ms. Jackson, and the violin fairy. Austin was embarrassed that he had allowed his violin to shrink to such a tiny size that he couldn't play it well anymore.

Then one day Austin was sitting in his room. Suddenly without warning, his cat jumped onto the table and knocked Austin's violin case over. His violin fell out and landed on the floor.

Austin was scared. He thought his violin had been broken. Thank goodness his violin was fine. He picked it up and glided his bow across the strings.

At first it didn't sound good. His tiny violin was hard to play. But he kept playing it. As Austin practiced his violin, he started to sound better. It was getting easier to play, and it was even fun to practice. Suddenly he could see himself on stage with the bright lights shining and the crowd shouting, "more, more!"

Every day Austin practiced his violin. His parents said, "You're getting so much better. We're so proud of you!"

"You are improving!" said Ms. Jackson. "You rock!" said Austin's friends. Austin held his chin up high once again. He wore a great big smile.

In class his friends said, "Look! Your violin is growing bigger!"

Everyone at school stopped talking about his amazing incredible shrinking violin. His classmates stopped laughing at him and making fun of his tiny violin. Austin continued to practice. He loved his violin. His violin continued to grow until it had reached its original size.

Austin became so good on his violin that Ms.
Jackson asked him to play a solo on stage for their
upcoming concert.

His dream of being on stage with the bright lights was coming true. Austin learned that if he practiced hard enough he might one day become a big violin star. Austin practiced his violin every day. He didn't want to lose his red violin and the beautiful music it made.

And that is the end of the amazing incredible shrinking violin because it never ever shrank again.

THE END

Song Titles

CD Track List

1. The Amazing Incredible Shrinking Violin (narration by Briana Middleton)

2. The Amazing Incredible Shrinking Violin (narration by Briana Middleton with page turn tones)

Children's Choir and Violin

3. A Violin Star

4. Play It Again

5. E String, A String

6. I Can Play My Violin

7. I Can Take A Bow

8. My Violin Teacher

9. My Violin Rocks

10. My Violin Is Never Gonna Shrink

11. I Love My Red Violin

12. I Can Hold My Violin

Violin Solo

13. A Violin Star

14. Play It Again

15. E String, A String

16. I Can Play My Violin

17. I Can Take A Bow

18. My Violin Teacher

19. My Violin Rocks

20. My Violin Is Never Gonna Shrink

21. I Love My Red Violin

22. I Can Hold My Violin

A Violin Star

Thornton Cline

Moderato

I'm go-nna be a vio - lin star. Up on stage in

front of the lights. They will cheer and clap for me.

I will play with all my might. I'm go-nna be a

vio - lin star. Wow them with all my songs.

I'm go-nna be a vio-lin star. Watch me take a bow.

Play It Again

Thornton Cline

Moderato

Play it a - gain. Play it a -

gain. Play it till it is right,

no more wrong notes for me. Play it a -

gain. Play it a - gain.

No scratch - ing, no squeak - ing. Play it till

it sounds good. Play it a - gain.

Play it a - gain.

35

E String, A String

Thornton Cline

I Can Play My Violin

Thornton Cline

Moderato

I Can Take A Bow

Thornton Cline

Cheerful

I can take a bow. Watch me take a bow. Peo-ple clap for me,

when I play my vi - o - lin. I can take a bow.

Watch me take a bow. I prac-tice, I play.

I sound bet - ter eve - ry day. I can take a bow.

Watch me take a bow. Eyes on me. Here I go.

One, two, three. I can take a bow. I can take a bow.

Watch me take a bow_____.

My Violin Teacher

Thornton Cline

Tenderly

My Violin Rocks

Thornton Cline

Gleefully

My vio - lin rocks! Oh how it

rocks! My vio - lin rocks!

It sounds so awe - some, I have so much

fun I could play it all day.

My vio - lin rocks! Oh how it

2

rocks!   My vio - lin rocks!

I can play fast and I can play it

slow.   I can play high and I

can play it low.   My vio - lin

rocks!   My vio - lin rocks!

My Violin Is Never Gonna Shrink

Thornton Cline

Brisk

I Love My Red Violin

Thornton Cline

I Can Hold My Violin Up

Thornton Cline

Biographies

Thornton Cline is author of four books: *Band of Angels, Practice Personalities: What's Your Type?, Practice Personalities for Adults,* and Cline's first children's book, *The Amazing Incredible Shrinking Violin.* Thornton Cline has been honored with Songwriter of the Year twice in a row by the Tennessee Songwriters Association for his hit song "Love is the Reason" recorded by Engelbert Humperdinck and Gloria Gaynor. Cline has received Dove Award nominations as a project writer and Grammy Award nominations for Music Educator. Thornton Cline is an in-demand author, teacher, speaker, clinician, performer and songwriter. He is a registered Suzuki violin teacher with the Suzuki Association of Americas. Cline teaches piano, violin and guitar at Cumberland University, Sumner Academy, Gallatin Creative Arts Center, Aaron Academy and Hendersonville Christian Academy. He lives in Hendersonville, Tennessee with his wife Audrey and children Alex and Mollie.

Susan Oliver is an award winning songwriter and visual artist as well as illustrator. She is originally from Orono, Maine and attended the University of Maine as well as Portland School of Art. Known for her wide variety of styles, Susan has exhibited her artwork and also worked as a graphic designer. Her painting, "Moonlight Seals" gained national attention in efforts to raise funds for Marine Animal Lifeline, an organization dedicated to seal rescue and rehabilitation. Susan now resides outside of Nashville, Tennessee where she continues to write music and design art work for album covers for various musical artists, as well as illustrates children's books. The Amazing Incredible Shrinking Violin is Oliver's first children's book published as an illustrator.

Briana Middleton is a junior at Ensworth High school in Nashville, Tennessee. She has been involved in a number of artistic projects, including Lifeway videos and a Ked's Campaign with Taylor Swift. She has also had her fair share of theater. In addition to her school performances, Briana attended the first ever Nashville High School Musical Awards and walked away with the award for Best Female Vocalist and All-star Cast Member.

Even with her accomplishments in theatre, Briana admits that her first love is music. She has been singing for six years and is heavily influenced by artists like Etta James, Florence Welch, Aretha Franklin, and Whitney Houston. She recently joined a Funk/Jazz band called the Broomestix and they play venues all throughout Hendersonville and Nashville.

This is the first narrative voice over Briana has done, but she hopes to do many more in the future.

Credits

Audrey Cline

Alex Cline

Mollie Cline

God

Ron Middlebrook

Clinetel Music

Centerstream Publishing

Hal Leonard

Susan Oliver

Briana Middleton

Lawrence Boothby,
photographer

Crystal Bowman, editing

Lynne Drysdale Patterson

Marcelo Cataldo

Parents of children

Kyle Gott

Children's Choir:
  Nora G.
  Cohen T.
  Ethan K.
  Laura S.

Sumner Academy

Cumberland Arts Academy

Cumberland University

Hendersonville Christian
Academy

Gallatin Creative Arts Center

Aaron Academy

More Great Books from Thornton Cline...

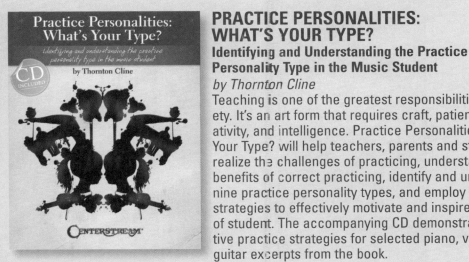

PRACTICE PERSONALITIES: WHAT'S YOUR TYPE?
Identifying and Understanding the Practice Personality Type in the Music Student
by Thornton Cline
Teaching is one of the greatest responsibilities in society. It's an art form that requires craft, patience, creativity, and intelligence. Practice Personalities: What's Your Type? will help teachers, parents and students realize the challenges of practicing, understand the benefits of correct practicing, identify and understand nine practice personality types, and employ useful strategies to effectively motivate and inspire each type of student. The accompanying CD demonstrates effective practice strategies for selected piano, violin and guitar excerpts from the book.

00101974 Book/CD Pack $24.99

Companion DVD Available
00121577 DVD $19.99

PRACTICE PERSONALITIES FOR ADULTS
Identifying and Understanding the Practice Personality Type in the Adult Music Student
by Thornton Cline
Did you know that your personality can affect the way you learn and perform on a musical instrument? This book identifies nine practice personalities in music students. Adults will learn how to practice more effectively and efficiently according to their personalities. A Practice Personalities test is included along with an accompanying CD.
00131613 Book/CD Pack $24.99

P.O. Box 17878 - Anaheim Hills, CA 92817
(714) 779-9390   www.centerstream-usa.com

Did you like this book? If so, check out this great book!

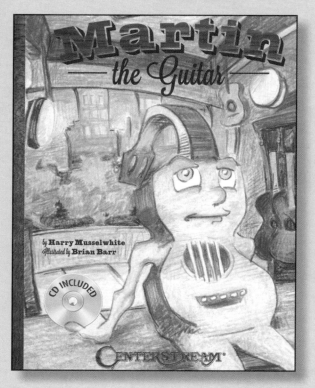

MARTIN THE GUITAR
by Harry Musselwhite

This charming children's story will delight music lovers of all ages. Little Martin the Guitar lives in Mr. Beninato's Music Store in New York City. He wants so much to be adopted and taken home by a fine musician, but the other larger instruments in the shop are always picked before him. Every night after Mr. Beninato goes home, all the instruments play for each other and compete for a place of honor in the shop. The large and loud guitar known as Big D always wins the contest. One night, Strada the Violin decides to step out of her special case and help Martin win the contest, and the two perform a duet that leaves the other instruments looking on with awe and admiration. Join Martin and all his friends for a CD of music from Mr. Beninato's Music Store! Performed on guitars, mandolins, banjos, and more, hear songs from the book entitled "Strada's Waltz," "Mr. Beninato's Music Shop," "Martin's Lullaby," and six more tunes made to bring a smile to your face and to set your toes tapping!

00001601 Book/CD Pack..$19.99

P.O. Box 17878 - Anaheim Hills, CA 92817

(714) 779-9390   www.centerstream-usa.com